You
Won't Remember
This

for Peter

friend of poets

Michael

YOU WON'T REMEMBER THIS

poems by

Michael Dennis Browne

Carnegie Mellon University Press
Pittsburgh 1992

ACKNOWLEDGMENTS

Some of these poems, or versions of them, first appeared in the pages of the following magazines and anthologies; I am grateful to their editors for permission to reprint.

Agassiz Review, American Poetry Review, Crazyhorse, Great River Review, Ironwood, Prairie Schooner, Sidewalks, Southern California Anthology, Special Reports: Fiction (Whittle Commmunications), *The Iowa Review, Tri-Quarterly, Virginia Quarterly Review.*

The Decade Dance (Sandhills Press), *Anthology of American Verse & Yearbook of American Poetry* (Monitor), *Annual Survey of American Poetry: 1986* (Poetry Anthology Press), *Light Year 87, 88* (Bits Press).

I am grateful to the Jerome Foundation, the Bush Foundation, the graduate school of the University of Minnesota, and the Loft-McKnight Awards for financial support, and to the Cummington Community of the Arts for some fine days.

Special thanks to Chester Anderson, David Bengtson, Louis Jenkins and Lisa McLean.

Publication of this book is supported by grants from the National Endowment for the Arts in Washington, D.C., a Federal agency, and from the Pennsylvania Council on the Arts.

Carnegie Mellon University Press books are distributed by Cornell University Press Services.

CONTENTS

4: You Won't Remember This

FOR PETER, MARY AND NELLIE

I

MENGELE

Don't tell me about the bones of Mengele,
the bones are alive and well.
Don't think to thrill me with tales
of the drowned bones uncovered,
the bones are alive and well
inside the sleeves of a suit this day
and carving out the figures of a fat check
or severing a ribbon with the ceremonial scissors
or holding the head of a child;
I tell you, the bones are alive and well.

Don't expect me to get excited
concerning the skull of Mengele,
the skull is alive and well,
the skull is asquirm with schemes this day
and low words are leaving it at this moment
and other skulls are nodding at what they hear,
seated about the world table;
I tell you, the skull is alive and well.

Don't bother showing me pictures
of the remains of Mengele,
the remains are alive and well
and simmering in our rivers
or climbing into our houses out of the ground
where they will not be confined
or sliding inside the rain
out of the summer air, oh yes,
the remains are even there, I tell you,
are alive, are well, are everywhere.

BREECH

We called and called but he did not come. We stared
at each other. So we ran looking for him,
twisting, panting among the trees, losing sight
of each other, making contact again, even colliding
once, more than once, sweat-stung, salt-smarting,
asking: Did you see? Did you? Was there anything?
It was when we were standing panting in front of
the same thick oak where we began that we saw him,
or saw his feet first, descending out of the tree
where he had been hiding, saw him sliding wordless
backwards, striped with blood, his skin creased
and cheesy, slowly, slowly, as the tree bark
yielded him, his legs, his buttocks, his little
wrinkled back, and at last the matted, clotted hair
on the back of his head, until, with the tree's
last effort and the wordless closing over of its bark,
he slid onto the muddy ground and lay there, lips
slightly parted, panting, and we forgave him.

BIKING ABOUT IN THE HOT DARK

This summer I dream of being
anywhere other than here
in the pitiful city, dream
of being no more than features
wandering on blue water, my pale
body broken below me
in blue water.

Those who love the night,
who come alive in the night, what
hope for them in that heaven
reputed to be light? But I
am not one of them, though I love
the leaves required to shine
under lamplight, though I know
these crickets consider themselves
the troubadours of night.

When the day comes, as it will
come, with its legions
of radiance, let night rub itself
one last time against the earth,
one long last cindering time
against the earth, then slither
with all of its secretive songs,
and be gone.

FIRST TEACHER

in memory of Christa McAuliffe

You had no plans to have your students scream
And wail and hold their heads in disbelief,
Whom you were primed to instruct from high in space
(O such a hook-up for New Hampshire).

Not quite the force of those explosions
In which the citizens of two far cities
Were vaporized, their outlines blasted onto
Walls and sidewalks, no, not for one instant

Beamed down upon the blue sea, not reflected
In all your human wholeness among vacationers'
Rentals, yachts meandering, charters
Heading out crammed with their boozy executives

On a spree. But suddenly you are equal
To metal, descending at the same speed,
Suddenly only wreckage, with which
The clear sky is fouled. Let the appalled

Weeping children be instructed by this,
That whatever the promises mother or father
Or teacher may murmur, it is possible to step
Through any moment's door and become air.

NORTHERN IRELAND DREAM

The child began to slap me.
Her hands grew larger, harder,
became a man's, a sapper's,
rigging quick traps. She whirled
about me, she spun, tossed
flowers on my eye-graves, tombed
me with slaps. When I tried
to speak to her, she exploded.

FORSYTH COUNTY

(civil rights march, Cumming, Georgia, January 24, 1987)

1/ RIDE

Riding MARTA Bus #4009 out of Atlanta,
86 souls on board,
including the driver,
including 38 standing.
If this were a ship,
we'd be standing in water.

Cracking jokes about dynamite,
passing on rumors,
the K-Mart all out of .22 ammo,
a special on white sheets
down at the KKK-Mart,
jokes about snipers,
wondering how soon before dark
we'll be out of the little town
we're headed for. Those pines,
those low hills suit a sniper
just fine. Settle down
with a deerscope, wait.

Squad cars everywhere,
uniforms on every overpass, troopers
holding back cars at the on-ramps.
500 buses taking three hours
to make 40 miles.
Remembering Washington, 1969, Nixon's
wraparound Greyhounds, nose to tail,
sealing the White House.

What time does it get dark around here?
How late are we running?

A man at the front saying:
"My little girl just turned six,
last year was the first time
someone did something to her
because she was black;
it blew her *mind.*

Another: "I work with these guys all week,
for years. I ask them:
will you be out there tomorrow
with rocks, with the rest of them?
They say: What do *you* think?"

The driver: "Up there on an overpass,
don't need even a brick on the windshield -
balloon full of water do the job."

How late are we running?

A voice announcing:
"Remember, non-violent.
Remember, non-responsive.
Remember, don't leave any money
in Forsyth County.
Stay away from Big Mac.
Don't go near the Colonel."

Someone singing: "Ain't gonna let nobody turn us around."
          Everyone: " Turn us around, turn us around."
Someone: "This little light of mine."
          Everyone: "I'm gonna let it shine."
Someone: "If I had a hammer."
          Everyone: "I'd hammer in the morning,
          I'd hammer in the evening,
          All over this land."

Singing, chattering, laughing, sweating,
silent, staring, coughing, praying,
and all of us, all of us, all of us,
Lord, Lord, Lord,
Leaning on the Everlasting Arms.

2/ WALK

We are here by permission of helicopters,
weaving, swerving,
five or six of them,
making close passes,
making themselves felt.

We are here by permission of walkie-talkies,
crackling, spitting,
voices barking from them,
voices murmuring into them,
by permission of hundreds of helmets
like low clouds,
by 2000 in full riot gear,
by permission of visors and clubs and barrels,
by holsters, by water-bottles, by olive-green,
by dull stares, bored stances, hands on belted hips.

We are here by permission of media,
the region, the nation, the planet,
by clicking, by whirring, by focussing
under thousands of lenses,
protection of microphone, notebook,
protection of paper, of pen.
By no permission of love are we here.
Injunction. Permit. License. Ordinance.
By permissions such as these we are here.

Some families, some single figures,
standing at the windows of houses
as we walk by, silent, arms linked,
seven or eight abreast
down the narrow two-lane toward
this unremarkable Georgia town,
some on the edge of their property,
leaning against a tree or a mail-box,
sometimes a woman,
sometimes a child or two,
waving shyly; *who are they?*
Could it be I see
my own face there?
Faces of family? Friends?

On the edge of town, a man
with white tape over his mouth,
holding a sign that reads:
I *LIVE* here.

We are thirsty, we are hot, we are hungry,
but when the talking's all done
we head for the buses,
we won't leave
any coin in Forsyth County,
the fast-food joints
anyway chained, dead-bolted,
chairs piled high at the windows and doors,
the ovens cool, vats of oil cool,
the slabs of beef and chicken and fish
laid out in rows, frozen, unseen,
in the vaults, the cool tombs.

DANDELION, MELTDOWN

(time of Chernobyl)

At first, the spectacular gold.
How fast it rusts to white
then is gone, ghost by ghost,
in a mere wind.

Let us go and sit with our old
bald mother the earth a while,
let her mumble and ramble, as she will,
of her skies and seas.

Bring the young.

LADDERS LYING DOWN

The roof patient with me,
the rafters tolerant.

But my ladders are in love with lying down.

Rain, and such a rain.
A downpour
beyond all the laws,
descending upon the old
ovens, the mossy freezers.

And my ladders all in love with lying down.

I dreamed I stood back to back
with a wise one; felt
the heat of that healer's body.
Cold, I could not turn.

And my ladders all in love with lying down.

If wood could rust,
these are my rusty rungs.
While from the orchard I hear
low groans of the apples.
Patient with me, the harvest,
the fruit tolerant.

But my ladders are in love with lying down.

NATIVITY TRIPTYCH, 1989

1

A cold wind. Mean. Down to the bone.
A father holding his son in his arms
in a doorway, sheltering him,
squinting into the wind,
the boy's large Mediterranean eyes staring out
over the wrapped-around scarf,
eyes like the smoulder of sun
near the horizon, late afternoon,
the small limbs shivering.
Would they like to wait in the warm car
that's parked close by, engine running?
"No, thank you, the bus will come," the father says.
As I turn the corner, his second "Thank you!"
rings out down the ordinary street.
Then the bus. Then they're gone.

2

The tree is in the house, the blue-green guest,
whom every morning the children run to hang
with a new ornament. Odor of sap
like an ointment upon the rooms.
This creature is steeped in a sheen
borrowed from sea, from sky.

What does the visitor need?
Gifts of water, daily, such as pilgrims
bring to a shrine a god may have graced,
gifts of attention, the silence in which
we close our eyes and breathe before it,
until our ribs are a Bethlehem,

our breath straw,
a bed of breaths where the infant heart
can dream, can grow.

Since we are not to see the spirit,
never a glimpse
of whatever there is within
that in spite of the bite of axes splintering the doors
endlessly proposes, endlessly flows,
then bring offering
to whatever appears before us
as sign of that spirit.

Children, some water for our friend.

3

You dreamed the angel said to the world:
you shall bring forth a world.
For all your shadows,
you are the chosen ground.
When even the dark pours down,
you shall bear. And fed, you shall feed.
This, and then more than this,
you dreamed, you dreamed, children.

You dreamed that the child whom no one could find
came home, you dreamed
the child of wind took form,
you dreamed the return.
You dreamed that the angers were done
and showed us their dust,
you dreamed that the prisons gave up
their condemned, as seas their drowned.
You dreamed, you dreamed, children.

And you dreamed that the lights
we've hung at our door,
the lights our neighbors have hung,
all the lights of the street and neighborhood,
that you love,
that your eyes and hearts are alert for,
were not merely the flowers of our favored town
but could be the company
encircling anyone's loneliness, could be
choirs of wheat that chant
down the echoing bellies of the empty,
the length of the promised world,
as the angel told.
You dreamed, children, you dreamed.

HEAVENLY PEACE GATE   (TIENANMEN)

People would come so close,
would stand and stare into my face
mere inches away, amazed
at my nose, my body hair.

Chang, my young guide, wondered
about that hair, wondered too
why I had never married, being
forty already, and so every day
weaker.

I remember the sound of the
Chinese thunder, remember
thinking it a different thunder
than ours, drier, a rolling
of jars down the air.

And now these printed images,
these grainy meanders of blood. Never
to gain entrance. Only
to be able to stand, face

pressed to the gates of paper,
panting, staring.

GULF WAR DREAM

my legless son arriving home from school,
demanding to know what's on TV, which cartoons,
rings under his eyes, his seven-year-old
face pitiless: *what's on? what's on?*

first, I say, first, before TV, tell me
how you are, give me a hug, did this
happen to you in school today? tell me,
who did this to you? look at me.

he doesn't want to talk about it,
doesn't want to look, to touch, it seems
the wounds are old, it seems he gets by
quite nicely on his hands,

and pushing past me toward the TV,
white-faced, raging: *what's on? what's on?*

MAY FOUR

for the students of Kent State

Green, if you can bear to be
on earth again, as if earth
wept up her longing in green,
rooms of longing broken open by rain,
if trees can agree to being
robed again in blossom, as though
all blood that has flooded the ground
these twenty years returns
twined with the rain into shapes
such as the seas only over
centuries of grinding can fashion,

then how will *we* not say
that these we meet to honor
have soaked our own speech and song,
say they live again,
cells of our syllables, climbing,
as second by second the breath
renews in us, the survivors?
Whoever remains, us, whoever
is spared, us, how not to say
we give out our lives
not in the name of our single selves
but twined with the silent ones,
as unbelievably we breathe
those breaths denied our sisters
and brothers of breath.

Whatever it is that wants
everything down, everything done with,
stripped, spoiled, the earth over,
the rivers rotten, the fields
scraped of their seed, the pitiable
cities silent, their throats

wrapped round by their own
corroded streets, whatever it is
that wants these deaths forgotten,
plowed under, whoever, whatever
infiltrates the rain, stamps
cancelled on the seas, whispers
into the ears of the trees lies, lies,
who shreds the secrets of ancestors,
entombs the very smoke of their fires,

let that not be ever the only voice,
let that not go unanswered,
unnamed, ever, not be our signal
sent either to distant stars
and worlds which may or may not
be living, or into those lives
that look to ours, the children,
those worlds expecting that seeds
of the believing, not the despairing life,
be sown in them.

Allison, Jeffrey, Sandra, William,
what to say to *them*, the children,
in your name, in our voices
your imagined voices feed?
Say, perhaps or at least, this:
that the earth is not over,
as late in the terrible century
the war is not over, that we
continue to breathe on the spark,
again, again, for them, as for ourselves,
all the while imagining flame,

say to these daughters and sons
whom you were denied, that into
the warring world where green
and rain and May can bear to be
daily we return, our voices,
which are also your voices, raised,
in anger as in wondering praise,
in the names of the children,
our inheritors, and in your names,
Allison, Jeffrey, Sandra, William,
which are our names also.

5/4/90   Kent

II

BASSWOOD LEAF FALLING

At first it is a hand
as it falls, a swimmer's, blue,
lazy, and then it is

a glove, a workman's, with
the marks of work on it - rips,
splits, stains, scratches, burns -

and then a document, the one
on which the names of those
to be reprieved are scrawled;

how casually yellow it wanders
down to drift into its place
among all the other permissions

asleep upon the earth.

POTATOES, OCTOBER

Potatoes, that's what I'm after
and that's what I find
with my fork, at the first turning
seven, red ones, all sizes.
Last night's hard frost above
was just a buzz to them.

Why are the crows suddenly calling
back down the hill?
Is the spud some god
to them? They can have
these green tomatoes instead,
frozen clear through but
convincing from a distance;
rare globes of jade.

Let the crows get down
on their stringy knees to these
while I help the seven spuds
make good their escape

into hot water.

HARVEST MOON

I thought you would be more
the color of crops;
I thought you might earn your name.
But if you entered a bar,
each livid face would turn
and stare at you.

Why do you sink your vast ghost body
so close to us? You seem about
to pry mere pines apart.
How near dare you?

You look like nothing to nourish us,
no muse nor mother
with your scabby seas.
But if you have something in you
for our curing, come down.

ROAD OVERGROWN

And so we startle up
a hawk, a huge rust-colored
owl, see bear scat,
and are stopped
by swamp.

Glenda, our frail neighbor, says
it never was much good,
that road; but with wagon and team
in the old days,
you could get through.

Like us she loves a day
like this, of sun and driven cloud
and striving leaves, but says
she fears what follows;
her old bones dread what breeds
behind those brilliant winds.

NICE AND SAFE

The trees impenetrable; his beam
bounces off blunt dark.
"Keep me nice and safe,"
loudly he says as we tackle
the black hill.

There's a space between bed and wall
he's wary of; worms there, maybe,
or shreds of the hangman's rope.
Our cat curled there sometimes
who's now four weeks gone into
the belly of some fanged thing.

He's heard the bobcat's howl.
When the grouse hit,
he ran out with me to see
the nothing-to-be-done.
He knows frost fixed the flowers.

There will be nights with stars
he likes for us to go
for hikes with flashlights.
But intolerable to him
if he were ever not sure
of me there, I of a sudden
plucked from his side,

and he
alone on that road.

DRIVING SOUTH, SUNSET, FEBRUARY

House on fire, but only the glass
Fence on fire, but only the wires

Horse on fire, but only the eyes

FOR JAMES WRIGHT

I have been jogging and this
is the halfway spot on the dirt road.
Before I turn for home
I stop to watch the pines,
to hear the wind in them.

There are ten - three groups
of three and four and three -
and behind them a slope, north
end of a neighbor's pasture.

Ahead, behind, the dry reeds rustle.
Weeks from now there will be
mud and redwing blackbirds here,
a trickling, a whistling.

Now close my eyes. Now hear the wind,
hissing a little with the needles.
Ten trees. Slowly the branches stir.
My fingers go into the *mudra*,
thumb and forefinger joined,
the other three fingers of each hand
loose, lying open.

Now open my eyes. There are the pines.
Now open my hands
from the *mudra*, let the ten fingers
flutter a moment before me,
then up, up -
over my head I see the butterflies.

Turn then, and begin to run
back down the road, into
the last of the great light.

3/80

PRIMITIVE

In a light rain he squats
in his yellow rain jacket,
digging treasures out of
the dirt road, filling
his pockets with gravel.

Near dawn we'd stared
at the spider webs stretched
in their thousands across
the swamp, strung
among twigs and notches
of dead trees.

Our thoughtless neighbors
are gone, their two
damn grimy hounds are gone
that ran at the car
every time. House's
locked, barn's locked.
It looked like they didn't
have much, and they're gone.

He thinks each stone's
a crystal; humming,
slowly he builds his treasure
out of the dull road-bed;
gold, his creases and canyons
shine.

Beat a drum, someone.

MATERNAL

Let the fly-catcher build
where she wants, where she will;
that bird is no serpent,
and our eaves hers.

While that other is locked
to an upper branch,
looking out, looking down,
listening as night comes on
for her fallen,

the light beginning to fail
and somewhere below in the woodland
her young hawk walking.

IN SUMMER

Hard on these summer mornings to tell,
While windows flicker and rafters weave,
While handles hover and shingles swim,
What's real, what's seem, what's maybe-believe.

Shadows and leaves and light are the villains,
That fever their murmurs along the floor,
That riddle these rivers across our drowsing,
That make us a daughter at our door.

WIND, FOURTH OF JULY

Wind does one thing with clouds,
    another with leaves;
the clouds go, go, go; the leaves
    strain but they stay.

By the time the wind
    can take the leaves
they're shattered and yellow;
    they whirl-a-whirl a while
but then sink,
    they're the ground's.

As fast as the clouds fade,
    fresh tribes arrive;
all of the wide sky's strung
    with their travelling.

You who once knew me,
    you might think that that's
where my heart was, high.
    But these days I declare myself
on the side of the leaves,
    which, for all that the wind
can tear at them,
    stay with their trees;

though their shaking's extreme,
    though their staying's wild.

THE HOUSE WITHOUT US

Creatures must surely come closer than now
as we sit in a circle of lawn chairs,
quiet under August stars,
some fixed, some falling.

Sometimes I'd like to be something
a little less than human,
to be able to watch
as the bear sways up
to rub his rump upon the siding,
to rub his shadow up against our absence.

Leaves, one day I'll be one of you
rather than even the most neighborly star,
nearer to those we'll have left
and all *they* love;
they too encircled under these same heavens
but in some later August of the world.

SNOW DOG, OLD DOG

1

These August, these September winds,
unlike the April ones;
the way the leaves begin
to strain in some tough gusts,
the way the lake can be glimpsed
through gaps, where before
none were.

2

He begins to be a ghost
at the feast of our lives.
Where we gulp, he sips.
Where we run, there he ambles,
limping, who had shown such speed.
But in place of the grace we have loved,
we praise these motions now,
which are the way he must go.
But I tell you, there are days
I could carry him home
all a white heap in my arms.

My old lamb wants to sleep.

3

His long dreams on the sofa lengthen.
I have wished, while he dreamed,
that I could pipe inside them such a tune
that all the vermin would follow me
out of the town of bone.

And often now in so deep a sleep
he does not hear the arriving car
nor my steps to the door,

who once lion-like would have been
at the window, paws on sill, swaying,
barking bright greeting.

4

I am hoping the sunlight will heal him.
Let light be lavished - I'll pay. Surely
we could, from the berries of these woods,
achieve some poultice. I'll not
ask the loon for his mad remedy.
Sand, he calls,
sand, he giggles,
pour sand.

5

He loves the river. He'd like to stand
drinking from it forever
as it runs sturdy around him.
He stands looking up at me,
looking as if to say: *Do not*
call me back onto land,
whereon I burn. Let me continue
in this element forever.

6

Even on cortisone, the stairs seem steep.
Fifteen. More stairs than you have years.
First you tack to one side,
then the other. That way you make it.
The first time I carried you up,
you grunted as I lifted under you.

They've shaved your left flank;

you wear a boot of your own white fur
at the base of the pink, boy-like leg.
The scar's extended, its sutures
closed over where they drilled you
in three places. "An interesting lesion."
Such visions of fresh child-flesh, Snow Dog,
under that wise old fur!

7

Of the cessation of breathing
on the long table.
Of the stilling of the inexhaustible breath.
Of one of the forms of beauty, an end.

I have not known how
to bear this except to have
taken note, to have
escorted this passage,
accompanying him.

He endured to an age which,
were he son of mine, would
have been cause for mourning;
with him, cause for gratitude.
I am grateful for him.

8

See now how these August, these September winds,
unlike the April ones, set some of the leaves
to straining, and how, through spaces
where before none were, we see
waters which were always near, but hidden,
in which one might stand forever.

WATERING

It is a timid rain, that leaves
the topsoil moist.
Go down an inch or two
and it is dust.

So you must drench and drench,
mimicking the heaven that cannot,
it seems, leave earth alone,
as if heaven itself took form
to stand there, watering.

When is it enough? For all
you can spill, more will appear
to be poured through you.
All the voices of the soil
require your pouring, require
such a rain as you
had not ever thought
to let fall. Many, multiplying,
are the mouths of the earth.

Can dry ground dream of rain?
What hope for the ground
without what it cannot dream of?
Then you must stand and stand
until all dreams of dust
are done, until
all you are is rain.

III

A VISIT

My parents visited me
in the form of a river;
I felt the force of that river's flood
up my spine, as though
my back were the socket to receive
my parents' double power.

I grinned like a madman in a gale.

Then my mother and father
began together to braid
the hair of my life behind me.

WEDDING FIGURES

This is not the best picture of him, she would say;
look at this one. He's more handsome here.
What is it about this one she didn't care for?
She looks utterly young, blithe, happy,
her lengthy dress has the folds of a silk statue.
Perhaps it is that he looks a little awkward,
that he is leaning a little to the left, into her,
he could be straighter, or perhaps
that the morning coat looks slightly too big for him
and the striped trousers are a bit baggy,
you can sense the pale, blue-veined legs inside,
and also that the right hand below the stiff cuff
looks rather useless, like an actor who doesn't
know what to do with his hand and lets it
hang, or is it that the wrist of the left hand,
at the end of the arm that's linked
through her right arm, looks skinny, insubstantial?
And everything of him is leaning a little
to the left, toward her, though I had never
noticed it till now, never looked closely,
and yes, the vest slopes from his right hip
at a slight angle toward his left hip, the left
shoulder is lower; why can't this man
stand straighter at the nuptial parade? And because
his head is also turned just slightly, the right ear
looks bigger, while the left is more discreet,
and the smile is even a little foolish, like
a country boy in town and over-dressed, and then
there's the small unnatural brightness where someone
has painted in the small gap between two teeth
on the right side of his mouth.

If you turn the picture over (and it is
a silhouette cut out of the original) the white
backing shows his lean absolutely clearly

pronounced, and you'd think that someone behind them
in 1936 would have checked at the last
minute, and called *straighten up, Eddie* but
there was no one. The eyes, the eyes of both of them
shine; hers are larger, rounder, something more
of a serene content, but his have a boy's
gleam upon the older face, he is really joyed
to be standing here by this woman, so joyed
he can't quite keep himself still, even though
he's been posed, and he's hopping a little
from foot to foot, just slightly, not detectably,
and the shutter catches him as he's just
shifted onto the left foot, he can't really quite wait
for the music to begin, and while she's standing
obedient and still before the instructions
of the picture-taker, he's started already,
and today, my dancing master, we've caught you
at your little game.

WILD AND CALM LAMENT FOR MY MOTHER

1: Mum Before Death Dream

I saw this dream, four weeks before you died:

You stood on the pebbles of a beach.
You said: "I don't want the sea to touch me."
And then: "I am curious about the fishes
but I am not curious enough.
The earth, the twigs, the ants,
these are my friends."

In the empty sunlit town where my father
is the cobblestones, you went girl-like,
rattling a cart. You said:
"My father and mother are dead
and I am dead too. Do come
and see me some time,
stay just a little while.

I am safe in the sunlight in the empty town."

2: Late Bird

Why is it the late bird who draws me now,
where once it was the early?

O early bird, I wrote and wrote of you
till perhaps it was tiresome.

But now the late bird sings and sings,
so heedlessly, into the arms of dark.

Night is no weight for her; she is freed,
I think, by the dark, or pours

more purely for knowing it is she alone
who continues, unseen.

I read, I write. Even when I turn off my lamp
and roll toward sleep,

she is still at her song.

3: The Night You Died

The night you died I dreamed
a banal sexual dream, which,
when I woke, reminded me
of my old faithless life.

Things you never knew I did,
trees standing in water.

In that same dark a bird beat
again and again at the window,
so that at first light we strung
red rags against the glass.

Huge, these robins.
Strange how, after all these years,
still I expect them
to be little, the English kind.

4: The Trees

All across the air I saw
the trees you sent, the forests
of England uprooted, hurled horizontal;

you had now no tender thoughts
for the nests and younglings,
you tore up the trees
and sent them. I saw them pass.

Not the doodle-bugs the Jerries sent
while we shivered under the stairs,
but the huge exposed
root systems of English
beeches and oaks, the stained
muddy turbines hurtling by,
Epping, Sherwood, the Forest of Dean,
the Atlantic just a ditch at your death
and they leapt it.

Sent me your seas too, roused, whirling,
chopped by the cleavers of winds,
sent me your low scurrying clouds,
a rushing of gangs and packs,
a trailing of torn bellies,
giblet gangs, gizzard gangs,

sent me your dissolving,
beamed out your dissolution
upon me, the one devoutly
wished for but feared and suddenly
here, here, the body
scarcely prepared as the spirit
adieus it,

sent me against all winds your weathers,
so that I guttered,
your rains so that I streamed,
poured out your mourning grains,
the barns at last broken open, spilling
the stored years,

sent your sad hours on me,
beamed me your grieving,

so that my hair grew long
in a day, so that I stopped
to weep on the doorsteps,
your features, so that for days
I went about widowed, bearded,
with your face.

5: *The Alleys*

Running the alleys. St Paul. Mid-June.
You're four days dead. No one
will know I am mourning you.

I love these concrete lanes, these
stained neglected zones where nothing's
discouraged, where weeds, where flies
can get an education, where whatever
is crammed beneath lids is urged
to bulge its own way out, where
leaves and vines mutter, multiplying,
where chained dogs moan or flaunt
their fangs or whine and piss
at the pleasure of somebody passing.

It is not stable, this weather.
Above, the frontier sky-towns,
not stable. Bruised light. An electric
thriving over us. Last night,
one storm, another, everything
shaking, streaming, shining.
Collapse of those towns, rubbling us.
And I run to the rhythms
of last night's storms, to the rhythms
of those to come.

At the little flat,
peaceful, in your nightgown,

your hand on your breast.
They broke in.

No one will know I am mourning you.
Not able to be there,
I run, to blame for these storms.

"She'd be mad if you came," said Angela.
"Besides, she's international now."

I remember your narrow home
in London, where the four sisters,
Winifred and Nora and Julie and Molly,
grew up learning to talk "nicely,"
and that you passed on to me -
"Not jography, darling, *g*eography."
And your prizes for elocution, for Shakespeare;
always you relished, always could retrieve—

>   *I know a bank where the wild thyme blows,*
>   *Where oxlips and the nodding violet grows.*

Sometimes I wonder where
my own voice belongs, on what
street, on what ground.

I remember the trip up to London
when Granny died, going for you
because of your operation, remember
Grandpa weeping and Granny laid out,
so little, so lined, her long gray hair
coiled as always behind her head,
and that low attentive Irish voice
gone forever from the chilled head
I bent to kiss.

No one will know I am mourning you.
Not able to kiss, I run

these New World lanes, between storms,

> *Over hill, over dale,*

past pails overflowing with outtakes
of lilacs,

> *Thorough bush, thorough brier,*

split baby shoes, ripped
cereal boxes,

> *Over park, over pale,*
> *Thorough flood, thorough fire,*

dull brown and green
of wine bottles,

> *I do wander everywhere,*
> *Swifter than the moon's sphere,*

and all over
the crushed, upended cartons of milk,
drained by the hungry mouths and discarded.

> *And I serve the Fairy Queen,*
> *To dew her orbs upon the green.*

6: Box

The box is not musical,
the box is nothing to listen to,
nothing to wind,
nothing to put your ear to,
to find
fresh batteries for,

no "Lavender's Blue Dilly Dilly,"
no "Away in a Manger."

In fact
the box
takes
its voices with it
into the ground,
in fact
the box
sinks
into the ground

with its songs,
with its bones,
with its songs.

7: Cemetery Photo

All those flowers
on and around the grave.

My sister writes: "Think instead
of all the people who were there."

Flowers wreathed into rings
and laid on the soil they rose from,

flowers with their perfumed faces
pressed to the mirror of earth.

8: I Should Bloody Well Hope So

You fell down; later, you wouldn't admit
you had fallen. Once you said:
"I always escape in my dreams."

Driving around England in the rented car:
churches, picnics, nice little pubs.
"I can't believe this is happening to me.
I feel as if I'm living
in some strange sort of dream."

Once you wrote poems. You said:
"I'm just going to sit down and let my words
come out the way they want to."

On the phone:
"I love you too much, you'll never know.
I love you to bits."

Of modern art:
"Picasso used to paint such lovely things,
but then he went all strange, poor darling."

At home: "I always see faces . . . in the fir tree
always, always I see a face.
When I sit outside, I see faces
in the clouds.
My chair is right opposite the clouds."

In the last weeks: "How strange life is.
It goes all the way down
to the beetle, everything
feeds on everything.

Sun . . . wind . . . trees . . . birds.
When your flesh rots away from your bones,
where do you go?"

"I love you, Mum."
"I should bloody well hope so."

9: No Dreams

Why haven't I dreamed of you?
Five months. Not once.

I *talk* to you every day,
parking the car, bringing
the grocery bags into the house.

Old corpse,
old starfish,
old arthritic bones
wrapped up in Weybridge,
old one of eternity,
why haven't I dreamed of you?

Passing that farm, I think
its leaning granary
must long to lie down,
lie back in the long grass
and be circled by swallows.

No use beseeching
the undemonstrative heaven;
not a wordy God, ours.

Mum of the spaces,
Mum of silences,
old continent,
old origin:

no dreams.

10: At Last I Dream of You

At last I dream of you.
It's been ten months.

I'm in front of a mirror,
I have your face, your lipsticked mouth,

and however I brush my hair
it will not flatten across my scalp

but stays high, yours.
And these red lips—

how can I possibly
go out like this?

11: *All Over. Fear No More.*

All over, the little flat,
where you felt safe, more or less,
days with the telly on,

to have people there,
the apple slices and barley water
on the table by your chair.

All over, the walls of faces,
the children, grandchildren, nieces, nephews,
the Sacred Heart, Our Lady of Lourdes,
Father Bertrand, whose death seemed to scare you,
Uncle Frank, whose death shook you,
Daddy, whose death uprooted you.

All over, the diminished life,
the clouds drifting or rolling
over the Surrey hills, the blazered
children chattering to school
and back from school,
the milkman, the postman, the knock
on the double-locked door ("Who is it?").

Fear no more
    the trip to the store,
Fear no more
    the afternoons, the years,
Fear no more
    the struggling up from the chair,
    the trying to get to the phone,
Fear no more
    the waking alone with pain,
    the dishes piled, the spiders
    sprinkling their blue silences
    about you.

    Old origin,
Fear no lonely more.

12: I'm Sorry to Hear Your Mother is Dead. How are You Feeling?

Inside the body
many miles of canals, minor rivers,
windings of weedy backwaters.
A punt sliding by, a slow skiff,
an angler dozing.

Plenty of quiet little pubs
in that land, where my parents
can sip their pints.
The children? They're around somewhere,
they're near, you can hear
their cries. They're happy.

I carry old churches inside me,
sweet air of incense from mass,
the kissing and lighting of candles,
swift whispered prayers, then out
into sun, or drizzle, or wind.
I carry that mother and father inside me,
I'm a hall of syllables
where their low voices are murmuring
secrets I've not forgotten.

In the tape of the service you can hear
the old hymns she wanted and got,
thanks a lot, Mum, not a dry eye
there, then, in the old world,
nor here now, in the new,
you can hear the voice of the celebrant,
Father Kemble, my old Chemistry teacher,

intoning over "the body of this our sister,
which we are about to bury,"
leading the farewell to
"our sister Winifred," you can hear
behind him the sounds of traffic
along Heath Road, Weybridge, where
the polished cars will soon creep,
left at the bottom of the hill,
right in a few hundred yards onto
the gravelled drive of the cemetery,

you can hear "may the angels bring you
into the arms of Abraham ...
till we all meet in Christ..." and the final
dogged playing of Brahms' St Anthony Chorale
which Daddy would have died to hear,
his organ, after all, *his* instrument,
and then the end of the tape, the hiss
and crackle of nothing left to record,
you can sit and listen to that if you want,
because who's to stop you?

Old loves, what do I say
but that daily I go back
to what you gave, say
it is given still, out of
an endless wellspring,
that wherever I travel
it is proper to talk to you,
as I do and will?

Whatever street I am on, the feeling
that somewhere you *are*.

These lambs about me, their leaping,
the wife I am learning continually
to love, if I cannot
name these amazements daily,
how am I your son? The days
ease into another summer,
old branches recover their green,
and these faces, in whom I see you,
lean, oh, eagerly, toward the world.
What I ask, old loves, of you,
is the courage, the praise
the difficult world deserves,
as we go on into whatever
our lives will become,
into its singing, which in us

you began.

IV

TO SHOW PETER THE WORLD

Are we, perhaps, here just for saying:
house, bridge, well, gate, jug, fruit-tree, window . . .

—R. M. Rilke (Ninth Duino Elegy)

It seems as if sometimes in sleep
the names drift off from their things.
The name-mist lifts. The things shine, clean.
On other nights the usual heavens
slide under and are gone.
New constellations gleam, suggestive.

It seems that I am bound to be
yet one more Adam, with my seven-month son;
not Lear, exhausted, bearing his daughter
at the very end of things, vowing
with all music what can never be, but
at the beginning, Peter, in truth
at the start of it all. *We two will sing.*

There are days, child, I have woken
ashamed of the names, wanting,
for your entering, fresher ones
for what you will come to know,
and what I must learn to do, all
over again, is trust the necessity,
the endlessness, the grace of our naming,
which is human, which is what we do,
and sound again around lips and teeth and tongue,
and roll again down bones and veins,
familiar syllables, yes, the usual ones,
until they assume the unknown again,
until no name's familiar, and learn

not only to wander with you
the present borders of our naming
but to be there to watch and listen
as you begin going on beyond,
making *your* names for the things, as
Peter shows Peter the world, this place
into which we have only brought you,
and in which we must leave you.

BY A WATERFALL IN WALES

for my six months' son, distant

Instead of writing words for you,
   as today I came to do,
I laid down my pens and book
   to climb the rocks by the waterfall,
there where the thick flood
   crashes and twists,
collapsing its sudden silver
   into shaking pools,

   as a boy would,
    as you-a-boy will,
    as I can still
   with my not-yet-old body,

until I was infant as you,
   there where you slide and grip,
clambering upon the milky body
   of her we love.

And instead of shaping a song for you,
   as I had meant to do,
long I sat to let
   all knots inside me,
those taut ones, loosen,
   until the only flowing
I could feel was the hiss
   of an innermost silk

   through the tunnels,
    down the caverns,
    the moss, the stones
   of my listening body,

from which, as out
   from among the limbs
of her your source
   you spilled glistening.

PETER AND THUNDER

Your face when you heard it. How you looked up.
How, crouched over toy parts,
suddenly you stiffened. How then you turned,
how you stared up in the direction
of the thunder. *They are at the gates.*
How then you looked at me, as if
I might send them away, as if with a few
low-toned, well-chosen words I could
send the thunder-gangs scuttling back
through all the holes in the sky.
As if there were no thunder deep
down in my own bones, no thunder
in yours, little son.

DANCING FOR HIM

He likes to watch us dance, we do it
for him, he laughs, we waltz
around him in the kitchen or polka,
leaping, through the living room, he
laughs, or cheek to cheek like
a dragged-out marathon couple we
slouch and stagger, he throws back
his months' old head and laughs.

What he'll remember of these times,
who knows? Maybe one morning,
waking from a dream of faces,
he'll turn to one beside him, saying:
"That's it! They used to dance for me!"

CHICKEN POX

His back in the bath looked like
the work of a make-up artist
preparing the little player for
"Revenge of the Farmyard," the scene
in which, naked, he must run
the gauntlet of mutant hens, or like
the shrapnel bites you sometimes see
on the evening news, on the limbs
of children in the Middle East.

When I tell a friend I feel ill,
he asks: "Have you had the Chicken Pox?"
And I say: "Oh, I think so. Surely."
And remember only one person knows
for sure, and could I get through
to her, wherever she now might be,
and were granted one question, that
wouldn't be what I would ask.

His back looks like some zone
of the moon, or like a missile-testing,
bomb-proving range of arid land
you drive by in New Mexico, the fences
taut and well-maintained, the tall signs
saying "Keep Away," warning of penalties
if you breach the site.

HIS TOYS

We planned to keep your first toys,
preserve them; one day,
when you were grown, lead you
to a secret closet, watch you
pull wide, amazed,
re-discover your treasures.
But we can't; you're eating them.

WHAT HE SAYS

"Abé, Abé," weeping,
for no reason I know,
for nothing we've done,
and "Abé" again, howling,
as we buckle him
into the car seat.

Then "Aja!" as he grabs
the ring of shiny colored keys,
and "Dattu!" as he crawls toward
the small giraffe fallen
to the floor.

At the funeral for a young man
killed,
"Gaaa!" he yelled
as the mourners rushed by,
"Gaaa! Gaaa!"

SMALL HOURS

When you were little you would wander
  into our room, into the wide bed,
blurry with night words, and for lack of space
  I'd leave you there, to murmur and toss
beside your mother blooming with your unknown
  sister or brother, and I'd go
stumbling to one of the beds you'd left
  where I'd lie, hoping to dream
a drowsy girl's, a drowsy boy's dream
  of half-waking and tottering toward
a slow easy wave where I
  was admitted, where into the swell
rolling and salty with sleepers
  I'd be taken, and all the while
the stars swaying on their dark webs, the planets
  flickering like quiet tongues
in the mouths of the small hours.

DAUGHTER SONGS

1: Three to Kiss

Sometimes when I come home
    Still I'll forget
Until I've closed the door
And kissed my two
    That now we're four

And so I'll cross the room
    And bend and kiss
Then stand and shake my head
Still giddy with the gift
    Then maybe kiss some more

2: Good Friday Morning, 6AM, Devon,
    Listening to Mary and the Blackbird

Even a father would not say
You cause the sun to clamber up,
All sinew, from the valley floor;
No, for no songs of yours
But chimed by them, he'll slowly rise
To roll the granite mist aside.
O even a father could not say
You cause the sun to climb.

3: Early Birds, Late April

Those early birds, they wake me still,
But now *inside* the window sill;
No more at song above green streets
But gurgling low between white sheets.
Time was, I'd waken with a smile
Then roll back into dream a while;
But now it's up and out of bed—
These birds need to be changed and fed!

TELEPATHY

Today I explained telepathy to you,
    and telephone, and television,
        on the way to day care,

and I said, sometimes when I'm at work
    I'll think of you,
        and if I could send you that thought with my mind,

you'd get it right then,
    and maybe you'd smile, stopping a moment at whatever
        you were doing, or maybe not

but just going on with it, making a mask out of paper plates
    and orange and green cards
        with markers and scissors and paste,

or screaming circles in the gym
    either being a monster
        or being chased by a gang of them, but still you'd get

the picture I was beaming
    and you'd brighten inside and flash me something back,
        which *I'd* get, where *I* was, and smile at.

That's telepathy, I said,
    pulling into the parking lot,
        looking at you in the mirror.

THE THINGS YOU THINK YOU HEAR

One night a wedding,
with bells,
but the street is empty.

One January
the watering
of a garden, even

the silky dripping
from leaf to lower
leaf.

In the library, late,
you think you hear
the opening of a gift,

a child's hands
rushing
through soft paper.

YOU WON'T REMEMBER THIS

for Peter and Mary and Nellie

1

You lift your arms to your head,
which looks so dark, then turn
to lie on your side, the fluid
swilling in your abdomen.
The radiologist says:

"Anything dark is liquid,
 anything white is muscle,
 anything gray is bone."

These like the moon pictures,
wavering, grainy, the lens
lurching, and again you turn;
that shadowy bulb is your head,
those snow streaks your muscles,
those blurred tundras your bones.

you won't remember this

At ten days
you look lonely.
You seem between countries.

You look at me briefly,
not with interest.
You give no sign.

I toss you shreds of song
to where you lie,
down in the cradle canyon,
looking up.

Remote to you my moon
drifts over the rim.

You lie,
looking up.

you won't remember this

Today your first injection,
and tonight you cry, your thigh
throbbing. Now you have fallen
asleep on my left shoulder,
lying across my heart.

you won't remember this

You don't want to go
to day care today; you weep,
you cling to my leg,
you roll your eyes:
oh no oh no; all the sorrows
of my mother in my daughter.

you won't remember this

I hear a moaning from upstairs;
slowly you descend—*whooo whooo whooo*—
over your head the nibbled blanket;
on the last tread trip, topple
—*oops! oops!*—
and I gather up my ghost.

you won't remember this

Yesterday you set up a stall on a table,
invited us to buy. "How much is *this*?" we asked.
"About ten hundred," you said, frowning
at a pair of plastic feet.

Daily you bring us gifts with a shy face,
and watch us while we open them—
say a box with a wooden lid and in it
your yellow hairbrush, scraps of paper or card
with your green and blue coloring on them—
they're maps, you say, of the ocean, the sky.
Sometimes pictures we've cut out for you
that now you give back, wide-eyed
at our delight at getting them from you.
Daily you assemble such treasures and appear.

you won't remember this

2

Cresting the stony hill, the edge of England,
            and there was the sea,
the holiday town our parents brought us to
            when I was fourteen.
I found the dunes where we'd tumbled,
            swam in those waves again,
the breakers forever rolling in
            from the new world.
Such a boy I was then, all aware
            of myself in the waves;
but now the salted element itself
            and look, so many the swimmers.

At the country pub, sitting
            on the same stone wall,
but now with Peter, six, and still
            the leafy pulse of wood doves—

Hoo HOO Hoo, Hoo HOO Hoo —
        I wonder how I could want them back,
who are done with the human.
        Let them go.
Hoo HOO Hoo. Hoo HOO Hoo.

Heading home, we'd drive the moth-thick dark,
        wind-burned and dreamy,
both of them leading us in songs,
        easeful baritone, meticulous soprano,
and we'd chorus on,
        the waves, the doves, the gulls, the hedgerows
flashing inside us
        as we slid toward sleep.

And here my mother's little notebook now,
        its English addresses and numbers,
("Is it alphabetical, darling?" I asked her.
        "*Alphabetical?*"),
her late night wartime notes to my father,
        (at last we're sleeping),
some of my father's letters to her,
        some to *his* father:
"As I walk the streets of the City—*your* city—
        when I hear old tunes, oh! in so many other ways
which my poor pen cannot describe,
        I think of you constantly."

Love beyond naming, what will we keep
        when we've let go of all remembering,
what can we know when we've relinquished
        all rooms, all limbs, all breathing?
Gardens of daughters and sons we've tended
        and must leave, remember?
Lips and foreheads we will still want to kiss
        when we've no mouths for kissing,
remember?

3

Night. Night light. Now you are sleeping,
far from our own childhoods, deep in yours.
Nothing, loves, to remember,
no day, no street, no sky,
only rooms scribbled on water,
voices chasing voices down corridors
of seas, all the old cargoes
rolling. Unless we become as you,
we won't enter.

In such a sleep as this,
when all day is forgotten and runs
like a river under the skull, dividing
and tumbling up a million tributaries,
when the air is all words and leaves,
the garages adrift, the old barns wandering,
and even the careful stones are unstrung,
then, mother, then, father, go into
the dream with them, where the grief
we are separate is not known, till even
Abraham is understood, who would have
let go his son.

As you laugh, children, as you cry out
in your sleep, as you are blind,
as you are ghosts to the day
(though I love the days)
as the tongue has nothing to tell,
slumped like a beast on straw,
as the wine of the crushed days
spills and the ripe clocks burst,
releasing their seeds to the air,
then like climbers roped by the silks
of sleep, fragrant with the dreams
and forgetting of those mists,
we wander together.

Unless we become as you, we won't enter,
who have forgotten what the world will be,
to swim with you that dark unmaking
where the new life forms.

4

Someone should tell the dreamer to rise.
A day's begun that needs you; stir the fire.
Sleepers for sure, and soon, will need you,
swaying or stumbling down the stairs.
Hoo HOO Hoo. Hoo HOO Hoo.
Liquid, muscle, bone. Hold them.
Go with them into the day.

EVENSONG

"There he is" he learns to say
when we glimpse the great sun burning down
toward the hill, and "There she is"
when we spot the pale enormous moon
floating low above the pines;
and over and over, swiveling his head,
he says it as I drive them both,
daughter and son, around the roads
until they sleep, so I can have
dinner and an hour alone with their mother.

Ahead in the shadows, two deer.
A little further, metal abandoned
in somebody's yard, auto parts
and ancient appliances, that later
the moon will make into something,
that same skilled stranger keeping us
company beyond the branches.

He wants to know why they share the sky,
and all I can tell him is it's a secret
we have to guess at as we go;
and "There he is" he says once more
as the hill prepares to swallow fire,
and "There she is" as she climbs the air,
and murmurs and murmurs until he sleeps
(and she already is sleeping).